10 thing
knowin

G000108973

THE OLD
TESTAMENT

**PHILIP
GREENSLADE**

CWR

Acknowledgements

I want to thank CWR for sponsoring this book – indeed, I am thankful to the Lord for what for me is now a 25-year partnership with CWR in Christian ministry. I am especially grateful to Lynette Brooks and the editorial team, notably Rebecca Berry, for their encouragement and expertise.

My friends, Trevor Martin and Stuart Reid, continue to be a great encouragement to me and I appreciate them more than they can ever know.

Above all, I want to honour my wife, Mary, for her sensitive and skilful input to all my books, not least this one. This is just a singular example of the way she has shown me love and unceasing support throughout our life together. In the fiftieth year of our marriage, I dedicate this little book to her with unbounded love in return.

I pray that what I have written here may stimulate you to further Bible discovery. I pray that as you read, study, and explore the Scriptures you may encounter the author and hear His living voice.

Contents

Introduction

Jesus had a Bible. He called it 'the Law of Moses, the Prophets and the Psalms' (Luke 24:44); we call it the Old Testament. Jesus was brought up to value it. He heard it read and later based His adult identity on it. What was said of one of His followers might well have been said of Him: 'that from childhood you have been acquainted with the sacred writings' (2 Tim. 3:15).

Jesus was literate, and read these holy Scriptures reverently and radically. He defined his destiny by them. Reading from Isaiah 61, for example, Jesus says: 'Today this Scripture has been fulfilled in your hearing' (Luke 4:16–21). According to the Gospels, He quotes or alludes to 23 books of the Hebrew Bible, including from all of the books of the law, from most of the prophets, and some of the writings. Deuteronomy, Isaiah, and the Psalms seem particular favourites, along with Daniel and Zechariah.

Jesus intensified and deepened the message of the law and the prophets, but He did not revoke or abolish them. Rather, He claimed – and His chosen witnesses did too – that they were fulfilled in Him. He was the climactic chapter of a long-running story in which God was the chief actor (see Matt. 5:17 and Luke 24:27,44–45).

So why do modern Christians so easily neglect the Bible of Jesus? In your own church, how much time is spent studying Old Testament Scripture, compared with the New Testament? Perhaps, without an adequate grasp of the overarching biblical story, we lack confidence in how to read or teach the Old Testament. We may then simply hold on to a few familiar passages or characters or Bible stories; Psalm 23 always, Isaiah 9 at Christmas, and perhaps Isaiah 53 at Easter. Then there's Moses and the burning bush, David and Goliath, and Daniel in the lions' den. Otherwise, we may steer well clear.

Are we intimidated by the fundamentalists on both sides of the creationist–evolutionist debate? Or embarrassed by the conquest of Canaan? Perhaps we have bought in to the misconception that the Old Testament presents to us a violent God of law and wrath, while the New Testament offers us a fatherly God of love and grace? Whatever our reasons, when we ignore the Old Testament, we sell ourselves short and miss so much of what God wants to show us about Himself; about His saving plans and promises set out in Scripture, which are 'able to make [us] wise for salvation' (2 Tim. 3:15).

This book is a starter kit to help you get re-acquainted with the Bible Jesus knew and loved, by looking at the Old Testament through the New Testament eyes of the writer of the letter to the Hebrews. His letter is based on a series of sermons expounding key texts, which show the provisional and preparatory nature of Old Testament events and institutions. These texts are, notably, Psalms 8, 95 and 110, and Jeremiah 31.

Let's hear how that writer sees it:

'Long ago, at many times and in many ways, God spoke
to our fathers by the prophets, but in these last days he
has spoken to us by his Son, whom he appointed the heir
of all things, through whom also he created the world.
He is the radiance of the glory of God and the exact
imprint of his nature, and he upholds the universe by
the word of his power. After making purification for
sins, he sat down at the right hand of the Majesty on
high, having become as much superior to angels as the
name he has inherited is more excellent than theirs.'
(Heb. 1:1–4)

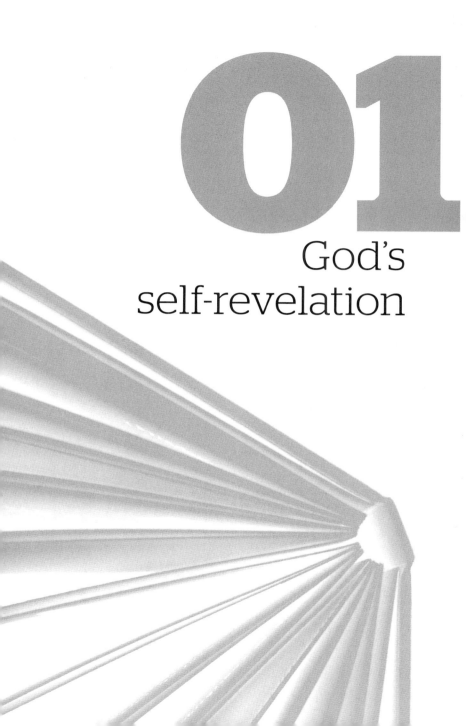

01

God's self-revelation

It is worth knowing that the Old Testament witnesses to God's self-revelation.

In the Old Testament Scriptures, we hear God speak. Here is the first keynote struck by the writer of Hebrews:

'Long ago… **God spoke** to our fathers' (Heb. 1:1)

That God has broken the silence and spoken to us is the foundation of biblical faith, and this foundation is laid down firmly in the Old Testament Scriptures. By the phrase 'to our fathers', the writer most likely does not refer only to the patriarchs, but to all the people of God. All Scripture therefore stands on this major premise: that God has made himself known to us.

God makes Himself known in two main ways: in creation, and in Scripture. Psalm 19:1–4 spells this out as follows:

'The heavens declare the glory of God,
and the sky above proclaims his handiwork.
Day to day pours out speech,
and night to night reveals knowledge.
There is no speech, nor are there words,
whose voice is not heard.
Their voice goes out through all the earth,
and their words to the end of the world.'

Listen as the psalmist connects this silent revelation of God's glory with the spoken and written revelation of God in Scripture:

'The law of the LORD is perfect,
reviving the soul;
the testimony of the LORD is sure,
making wise the simple.' (Psa. 19:7)

What we have here, neatly joined together in this psalm, are two aspects of God's revelation – two 'books', as it were.

> - Verses 1–6 tell us to 'read' Book One, the book of creation, which gives general revelation of who God is through what He has made.
> - Verses 7–14 celebrate Book Two, the book of the covenant – that special revelation in which God speaks to His covenant people, Israel, now recorded in the Scriptures.

Notice how Paul draws on both 'books' in Romans 1:19–20 and Romans 9:4–5.

What is crucial to grasp at this point is that Book Two takes precedence over Book One. Only in the light of God's covenantal revelation in Scripture can we name the world as creation, or name the creator and His glory, which it displays. The visual needs the verbal. For sure, God has not left Himself without a witness in the good things of creation (Acts 14:17). But this 'revelation' only calls us to account and summons us to recognise God. It is not, apparently, enough to save us. For that we need the word of the gospel (see Rom. 1:16–20).

God reveals Himself *without* words in the things He has made, but we can only know this because He tells us with words. God surely shows His glory and faithfulness in the wordless speech of the beauty and regularity of the sun, stars, and moon. But only by the spoken and written Word of God (such as Psalm 19) are we taught to see such things.

Created things are not an end in themselves; they illuminate their creator. Imagery from the created world, therefore, abounds in Scripture. So here, in Psalm 19, the regularity of the sun rising and setting echoes the faithfulness of God. Scripture enables us to realise that even rocks are made in part to show us how rock-solidly reliable God is:

'Let the words of my mouth and the meditation of my heart be acceptable in your sight, O LORD, my rock and my redeemer.' (Psa. 19:14)

When Moses gives the second reading of the Torah (Deuteronomy) on the verge of entry to the Promised Land, he reminds the Israelites of the foundational event of Sinai. There, he says:

'The LORD spoke to you out of the midst of the fire. You heard the sound of words, but saw no form; there was only a voice. And he declared to you his covenant, which he commanded you to perform, that is, the Ten Commandments' (Deut. 4:12–13)

Moses is said to have challenged the people:

'Did any people ever hear the voice of a god speaking out of the midst of the fire, as you have heard, and still live?' (Deut. 4:33)

And they had been tested in the wilderness period:

'that he might make you know that man does not live by bread alone but by every word that comes from the mouth of the LORD' (Deut. 8:3)

Israel's greatest privilege, as Paul saw it, was to be the steward of the 'oracles of God':

> 'Then what advantage has the Jew? Or what is the value of circumcision? Much in every way. To begin with, the Jews were entrusted with the oracles of God' (Rom. 3:1–2)

Or, as Eugene Peterson translates in *The Message*:

> 'So what difference does it make who's a Jew and who isn't, who has been trained in God's ways and who hasn't? As it turns out, it makes a lot of difference—but not the difference so many have assumed. First, there's the matter of being put in charge of **writing down and caring for God's revelation**, *these Holy Scriptures*'
> (Rom. 3:1–2, emphasis added)

Defined mystery

Now, of course, the language of God *speaking* words from *His mouth* is picture language. God is Spirit and has no anatomy. To speak as if He has is called 'anthropomorphism' – talking of God in human terms. The fact that God Himself sanctions talking about Himself in this human fashion speaks volumes for His grace in stooping to our level of understanding. Furthermore, it emphasises His strong desire to communicate and connect with the human beings He has created.

At the very least, the fact that God *speaks* reveals Him to be a personal God, and not a mere cosmic force. It shows Him to be a God who is intent not on imposing His will, but on forging a relationship with us, as the use of covenant language confirms.

God speaking of Himself to us does not, of course, exhaust

His mystery. But He becomes a *defined* mystery. As the Scripture puts it:

> *'The secret things* **belong to the LORD our God,** *but the things that are revealed belong to us and to our children for ever, that we may do all the words of this law.'*
> (Deut. 29:29, emphasis added)

Drawn into the drama

Our confidence is not that we know everything there is to know about God, but that what God has revealed to us is more than sufficient for our life and salvation, and will never be contradicted by what we do not know about Him.

Note here the mention of the law (the Torah). The word 'law' might have strongly negative connotations for modern Western ears. We might think it sounds legalistic and confirms in us the fear that God exists only to cramp our style and restrict our freedom. But the truth is quite the contrary: 'law' or 'Torah' is best interpreted as God's 'teaching' or 'instruction'.

This certainly implies that it is something to be done or adhered to. But God's 'teaching' is much broader than just commandments or rules. It includes the founding stories of the nation's patriarchs before the Exodus, and also the handed down stories about the creator's design for His world.

To obey this teaching is to respond by allowing ourselves willingly to be drawn into the drama as God's partners, and so freely and joyfully to participate in what He is doing on the earth. God's revelation evokes our response. And this is the crucial starting point for us.

Just over a century ago, when European Christendom was shaken to the roots by the horrors of the First World War, a young Swiss pastor, Karl Barth (who later became one of the most famous Christian theologians of the twentieth century) announced himself as wanting to reintroduce people to the 'strange new world within the Bible'. Barth was reacting sharply to the anaemic liberal theology in which he had been schooled. A mentality of 'it's nice to be nice' didn't cut it in the trenches of the Somme. What Barth felt the Church desperately needed to do was once again to take the Bible seriously as God's self-revelation:

> 'It is not the right human thoughts about God which form the content of the Bible, but the right divine thoughts about men. The Bible tells us not how we should talk with God but what he says to us; not how we find the way to him, but how he has sought us and found the way to us; not the right relationship in which we must place ourselves to him, but the covenant which he has made with all who are Abraham's spiritual children and which he has sealed in Jesus Christ.'[*]

Here is the big issue – the one that still challenges Christians whether they style themselves as liberal or evangelical – God has revealed Himself in and through the Scriptures.

As you read the Old Testament, listen for the voice of the living God.

[*]Karl Barth, *The Word of God and the Word of Man* (London: Hodder & Stoughton, 1928), pp28,43.

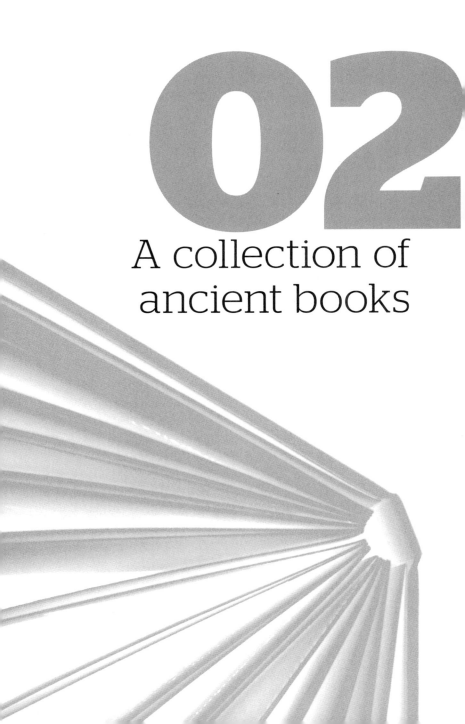

02

A collection of ancient books

It is worth knowing that the Old Testament is a collection of ancient books emerging over many centuries.

> *When God spoke to the 'fathers' it was* **'Long ago***, at many times'* (Heb. 1:1)

The only words of novelist L.P. Hartley to have made it into the *Oxford Dictionary of Quotations* is the oft-cited opening to his novel *The Go-Between*: 'The past is a foreign country; they do things differently there!'*

So it is with the Bible. It was spoken and written 'long ago'. When we enter it, we plunge into a 'foreign country' of ancient cultures and customs. We discover that its truth comes to us clothed in the way people thought and expressed themselves at another time and place. So how might we negotiate the strange world of the Bible? Two connected points can be made here: respect the context, and appreciate God's accommodation to it.

Respect the context

As far as we are able, let's try to respect the original context of what was said or written or recorded.

Nothing in the Old Testament was written *to us*, but to another audience at another time in history. It was certainly written *for us* – as Jesus and the apostles make clear – but it was addressed to other people at another time. This was 'long ago' (even more so for us than the author of Hebrews) to a distant audience in an ancient culture.

The Bible is not a flat book that can be ransacked for abstract principles using texts taken out of their context. Our first concern in interpretation therefore is to try to understand what was being said to that people group, in that specific situation.

> The old adage remains true: 'a text without a context is a pretext'. In approaching this ancient book or collection of books our first rule of thumb is: contextualise, contextualise, contextualise!

Appreciate God's own accommodation to the context

In approaching Scripture, it is helpful to remember that in His wisdom and humility, God has allowed the way in which His revelation is received, recorded and transmitted to be coloured by the cultural norms of the day. God's Word is usually counter-cultural. But to underline what we said earlier, its truth comes to us clothed in the thought-forms, imagery and idioms of another time and place. This is God's gracious condescension to us, stooping to speak to us at our level in down-to-earth and homespun language. Surely, an anticipation of the incarnation.

Take, for example, the areas of history and science. First, a word about historical reporting. Some believers have fought unnecessary (and usually futile) battles to prove that every single feature of every story in the Bible must have an actual factual reference outside the text in recorded history. Someone today, no doubt, is still looking for the ark on Mount Ararat. But for one thing, this gives too much credit to recorded history anyway: all history is selective and partial. Ancient narratives did not conform – nor should we expect them to conform – to modern ideas of empirical observation and objectivity. (As if only what can be accessed by recording equipment and film cameras is trustworthy.)

The ancients thought differently. They put much greater stock on what message was being conveyed by the stories they told. They trusted the role of eyewitnesses and the traditions of oral storytelling. This approach is usually termed 'historiography'. Nothing in such a method prevents God speaking truth through it – any more than it did Jesus when He taught using parables.

Secondly, what of the contested area of science? Misunderstanding here is surely the cause of much unnecessary conflict between faith and science. But here, too, let's appreciate God's willingness to accommodate Himself to the way different eras access truth. As we have said, when we approach the Old Testament, we need to give respectful attention to the cultural context in which God spoke or acted – in this case, the world-view of the Ancient Near East. Failure to acknowledge this leads to increasingly desperate literalism.

As an example, let's consider the opening chapters of Genesis. If you were to study the cosmology of the Ancient Near East – such as its three-storeyed cosmos, a water canopy looming over the earth, moons that hang like lamps in the sky – you will soon realise that God is not in the least compromised or embarrassed by revealing His truth through the imagery and concepts familiar to His intended audience. Genesis was never intended as a science textbook in the way we might wish it to be in the twenty-first century. In revealing His creatorship and our human vocation in His creation, God accommodated Himself to the cultural context of the time.

God does not demand of His earliest hearers or readers all kinds of knowledge about how the world works – knowledge that only later generations might be able to understand – and

He risks His reputation in doing this. He opens Himself to criticism from later and more 'enlightened' generations. Time and time again, God graciously condescends to His people's current levels of understanding and faith. We can be grateful He did and still does.

Find out as much as you can about the original context.

*A. Norman Jeffares and Margin Gray (Eds.), *Collins Dictionary of Quotations* (London: Collins, 1995), p308.

03

A partial, provisional and progressive revelation

It is worth knowing that the revelation God gives in the Old Testament Scriptures is partial, provisional and progressive.

*When God spoke to our fathers it was 'Long ago, **at many times** and **in many ways**... by the prophets' (Heb. 1:1)*

In past ages ('long ago'), to the patriarchs ('our fathers'), by the prophets...

What is it about alliteration that attracts preachers? No, I'm not talking about me, but the writer of the Letter to the Hebrews. He uses no fewer than five Greek words beginning with the letter 'P' in his first sentence alone. There are two 'poly' words – *polymeros* and *polytropos*, rendered in our English version as 'at many times' and 'in many ways'.

First, the word translated 'in many times' should more accurately be rendered 'in many parts'.

Here is a reminder of something worth knowing: that in the first stage of God's revelation of Himself, He did not disclose everything at the same time. Rather, for His own good reasons, He spoke here and there in different eras, giving fragments of truth over time. This has several fascinating implications.

What was revealed in the earlier phase of divine revelation was **partial**

What went before was fragmentary – parts of a jigsaw, each of which is true, but needs the other pieces for the whole picture to emerge. Crucially, as with a jigsaw, it is only when we see the whole picture on the box that we can truly see how the pieces fit together.

Among other things, this leads to what is currently known as 'intertextuality' – the way in which later texts not only quote but allude to and echo earlier ones, as in a symphonic arrangement. The passage of time is part of this process. We do not know how much of the 'Five Books of Moses' (Genesis, Exodus, Leviticus, Numbers and Deuteronomy) Moses actually authored. Being literate and educated, Moses may well have put quill to scroll. But what is clear is that Moses became the fountain-head for the final form taken by the books that are associated with him, and which carry his signature authority into future generations. A Mosaic tradition, if you will.

We see a similar thing with the 'Davidic' Psalms. David did not compose all of them, but they are associated with him having been inspired by his worship – so David is often the yardstick for God-endorsed worship. Similarly, Solomon is identified with the Wisdom Literature regardless of whether he authored it all. In each case, the continuing authority of these texts partly stems from their association with earlier iconic figures.

This is likely what we see with Isaiah (though this is a vexed issue). Though the great eighth-century prophet gave rise to a book that bears his name, it is arguable that later sections (notably chapters 40–66, which speak to a situation 150 years after the prophet's death), originate from what we might call 'Isaiah's prophetic school' (as Isa. 8:16 suggests). In this case, the phrase 'in many parts' may point to a long process providentially supervised by God, through which various scribes and students and editors compiled the complete Isaianic collection, themselves guided by the same Spirit as the original prophet himself. In the case of the book of Isaiah it is impressive to see how the later prophecies mirror the earliest ones, and how the whole thing hangs together.

More importantly, the phrase 'in many times/parts' reminds us that what went before in the Old Testament is *fragmented* revelation – not *final* revelation.

> For example, not everything we are meant to know about creation is found in Genesis 1–2. We need to add in other and later creation accounts such as Job 38–41, Psalms 8 and 104, and even more so, John 1 and Colossians 1.

What was revealed was **provisional**

Earlier facets of God's self-revelation do not tell the final truth about a matter. Some aspects of biblical teaching are superseded (for example, the need for circumcision as the marker for belonging to the people of God). Others are specific to context (such as the offering of Isaac, or the conquest of Canaan) and are one-off events not intended to be repeated.To put this another way, God's self-revelation in the Old Testament Scriptures is *provisional*.

This applies eventually to the central issue of debate in Paul's letter to the Galatians – the relationship between law and grace. Paul repeatedly argues, in terms of timeframes, that promise precedes the law. Then he argues that the law did govern believers 'until… the time for the offspring of Abraham to inherit the promise… until Christ came' (see Gal. 3:19,24). From then on 'the law', while still good and a true revelation of God's will, is incorporated in Christ and operates in the life of the Christian believer in a different way (see Rom. 8:1–4).

It is arguable that later scriptures within the Old Testament itself show Spirit-inspired adaptation and development of truth. This usually occurs in order to reapply the previous revelation to new circumstances, or to correct misleading interpretations of it. We can see this happening in the book of Deuteronomy (literally meaning 'second law'), which shows us Moses reaffirming the Torah, given once at Sinai, for the benefit of the generation poised to enter the Promised Land.

Within the Old Testament itself, we find truth emerging from disputation and dialogue between God and His people. As Abraham bargained with God over Sodom, so later Moses fiercely disputes with God after the incident with the golden calf, and mercy triumphs over wrath. And all this is how God intends things to be – one of the 'many ways' in which He speaks. Throughout the Old Testament we find counter-testimony and argument – all of which, in the providence of God, makes the truth clearer. This is especially memorable in the book of Job, which, among other things, dramatically serves to correct misuse of previous revelation – in this case, the book of Deuteronomy.

Job's friends had turned the Deuteronomic covenant into a cast-iron law, admitting no exception. If you did right, you prospered. If you did not prosper, things went badly for you. This is true, most of the time – but not always. Job rightly protests that his misfortunes are not the result of his sin, and God agrees with him. God takes Job's side against the crude prosperity-teaching of his so-called 'friends'.

Even the book of Proverbs can be perverted in this way and its wisdom lost. As David Hubbard puts it: 'Proverbs says, "These are the rules for life. Try them and you will find they work." Job and Ecclesiastes say, "We did, and they didn't!"'*

Proverbs, it seems, are not predictive or mechanical rules for living. They are words of wisdom appropriate to certain situations. What may be wise in one situation might be unwise in another.

Proverbs 26:4–5 is a case in point:

> *'Answer not a fool according to his folly,*
> *lest you be like him yourself.*
> *Answer a fool according to his folly,*
> *lest he be wise in his own eyes.'*

The second word of wisdom does not contradict the first: each is true in its own circumstances. The beginning of wisdom is not swotting up on the seven principles for living, but *the fear of the Lord*. In relationship with Him, we learn the wisdom of how to apply which proverb to which situation. We come to realise that the Bible has its own in-built checks and balances to help us hear the authentic voice of the God who speaks to us in and through it.

What was revealed was done so **progressively**

God's revelation in the Bible is *progressive revelation*. It unfolds over time and is not given at the start in its entirety. This certainly does not mean a progression from the less true to the more true, or from the less worthy to the more worthy. The author of Hebrews is insistent that if there is a progression from the Old Testament to the New Testament it is not from the bad to the good, but from the good to the *better*. But progression there is: like a snowball gathering size, so biblical revelation, in both word and deed, grows and swells as each stage of revelation gathers up and builds on what has gone before.

As Jim Packer summarises it:

> 'The historical process leading to Christ was progressive in the sense that one thing followed another until the climax came. God chose a man, made his family into a nation, gave that nation a land, gave them a religious culture in which prophets, priests, and kings were leaders and sin was highlighted as the hindrance to fellowship with God, and out of the frustrations of their national life raised their minds to a messianic hope. All this was a progressive preparation for Christ.'[**]

When assembling your biblical jigsaw, make sure you are working according to the picture on the box.

[*]David A. Hubbard, *The Wisdom Movement and Israel's Covenant Faith* (Tyndale Bulletin 17, 1966), pp3–34.

[**]Jim Packer, *Honouring the Written Word of God* (London: Paternoster Press, 1999), p91.

04

God reveals Himself in many ways

It is worth knowing that in the Old Testament, God reveals Himself in a variety of ways.

God reveals Himself **'Long ago... in many ways'**
(Heb. 1:1)

The overall sound made by a choir usually moves me more than solo singing does. I find that choirs move me deeply, whether Welsh male voices or Bach's Oratorios. And so it is for me with the Bible. Scripture is a choral masterpiece. It is not a monotonous, one-note dirge nor a cacophony of clashing ideas, but rather, it is polyphonic; many voices, many parts, singing from the same hymn-sheet of God's redeeming love and saving story.

This brings us to the second of our two 'poly' words. Having looked at the first (translated 'many times' or 'many parts'), let's look at the second, which is very important to consider if we want to understand the Old Testament: 'in many ways'.

It is clear from reading the stories of the fathers and the prophets that when God spoke to them they were fully engaged with the revelatory process. They were not passive conduits through which truth simply passed. They each had their own distinctive voice.

One thing that stands out from these ancient patriarchal stories is how closely God involves Himself in the often turbulent relationships with His people. The picture that emerges is not that of a distant deity who rules His world dictatorially, unmoved by His creatures' plight, but rather we see a God who encourages dynamic dialogue with those

He calls to partner with Him, as He did with Abraham. Jacob wrestles with God. The very name Israel means, 'I have striven with God and prevailed'!

The prophets too were equally engaged. They were fiercely (and often painfully) involved in the process of receiving and transmitting truth from God. Hosea is told to marry an unfaithful woman to embody God's Word to Israel. Ezekiel is told not to mourn the death of his beloved wife and engages in some bizarre street theatre to get his message across. Jeremiah feels and shows the pain of God over what is happening to his people. The supernatural finger-writing of Daniel's divine graffiti is an exception to the rule. But almost always, God speaks through human hearts and voices, often with bodily effects and always with full emotional immersion. This too is a prophetic signpost to the incarnation.

Such close divine-human interaction fits with what we noted earlier. As we saw, it is part of the genius of biblical revelation that God freely condescends to communicate with us in the thought forms and idioms of the cultural context in which He wishes to speak.

This is equally true of His choice of spokesmen and women for His truth. Those who spoke or wrote God's Word (or edited it into book shape) were obviously literary craftsmen and women. God chooses to speak through His servants – without overriding their individual personalities, but utilising their natural abilities and particular gifts. This fact alone makes the Bible fascinating, rich, varied, and multi-faceted. We can be thankful that God did it His way.

Be sensitive to literary genres

One important implication of the fact that God spoke in 'many ways' is that, in approaching the Old Testament, we need to appreciate the various genres of literature in which it is written.

'Don't we have to take the Bible literally?' Well, yes and no. Yes – if by 'literally' we mean to take all that God says in the text seriously. But also no – not if it means treating the Bible as a flat book, such as a collection of recipes or a kind of divine *Yellow Pages*. We are to take the Bible literally but not 'literalistically' – that is, we are to treat the Bible *literarily*, with careful attention to the *kinds* of literature or literary speech-patterns through which God speaks in different parts of Scripture. With that in mind, let's briefly reflect on the artistic styles or forms in which the biblical truth is clothed.

God's revelation in the Old Testament is offered in 'many ways' and so we need to:

Recognise the different types of literary genres used in the Scriptures – story, poetry, law, teaching, proverbs, songs, visions, sermons, letters, and apocalyptic. In only a few of these literary forms is truth reducible to propositional statements. Most genres allow truth to impact our minds and hearts another way.

Realise that truth can come in non-literal forms. And 'non-literal' does not mean untrue! Arguably, this could apply to the story of Jonah or some aspects of the opening chapters of Genesis. It is certainly true of the parables of Jesus.

Respond in the way the particular genre evokes (at least initially). Applying Scripture to everyday life is a skilful art because the Bible (in this instance the Old Testament) approaches us in a variety of ways.

How might this work?

Teaching

The Old Testament is Torah; instruction or teaching. It therefore works didactically, comforting us, but with tough truth; confronting us with covenant claims with a view to shaping a people fit to share God's story. When Scripture is in the mode of direct teaching and address, it means that *I am commanded*... and the Word is intended to be obeyed or practised so that we become doers of the Word. Only with Jesus and the coming of the new covenant arrangement will it become clear how this finally works. But the 'obedience of faith' is still the desired outcome (Rom. 1:5; 10:4).

An intriguing similarity has often been noted between the form in which God's covenant with Israel is couched, and the form of those ancient treaties imposed by overlords on their citizens. Such treaties follow a set formula, broadly mirrored, for example, in the book of Deuteronomy:

- A historical preamble outlining how the two parties have come to have this relationship and who is Lord in it (chapters 1–5)
- A list of stipulations spelling out the accountability of the junior partner (chapters 5–11)
- More specific rules detailing the ethical rules and responsibility governing the covenant relationship (chapters 12–26)
- Rewards and sanctions for treaty-keeping or treaty-breaking usually expressed as blessings and curses (chapters 27–30)
- The calling of witnesses to the treaty and how the treaty can be perpetuated into the future (chapters 31–34)

What do we gain from knowing this? If nothing else, that a covenant relationship with the one creator God is greatly to be cherished, and that breaking covenant, therefore, is extremely serious.

We learn that covenant with God is not a negotiated settlement, but one in which the Lord sets the terms because He knows what is best for our human freedom and flourishing. We could even imagine the bookends of John's Apocalypse standing in for the whole of our Bible as a covenant charter (see Rev. 1:3; 22:18–19).

Narrative

Not every part of the Old Testament is narrative in form, but it can be argued that every part of it presupposes and depends upon the redemptive story underpinning it. How does truth in this form affect us? By its very nature, the story – in its literary form of narrative – seeks to allure us and draw us into its own dynamics. By responding, we begin to indwell the story the Bible tells. That God-breathed story invites me into its workings so that I find myself involved and willing to go where the text takes me. What part do I play in God's story?

The Bible as narrative works dramatically, drawing us – by history and Gospel – into the redemptive story of God. No one exemplifies this better than Ruth, whose story is a bright light in very dark days at the end of the period of the Judges.

The chroniclers of biblical history were less interested in a kind of historical archaeology of past events and more interested in their theological significance and redemptive meaning. Often a pattern emerges. First the revealing word, then the saving event that confirms it, then further words that interpret the event.

Wisdom

The classic wisdom literature of the Old Testament – including Proverbs, Job, Ecclesiastes and other similar parts of Scripture – is meant to evoke its own response. Wisdom teaching encourages us to ask questions; to be curious about the natural world. It invites us to marvel at a sacramental universe in which God's grace and glory seep through every seam. It shows us how to respond wisely and with wonder at the micro-level of our own detailed daily lives. Fearing the Lord 'wises us up' when it comes to knowledge, understanding, folly, speech, emotions, family relationships, money, eating and drinking.

As wisdom, the Bible works reflectively making us ponder the meaning of life. It inspires science and discovery, exploration and poetry. Biblical wisdom prepares us to face the reality of the paradoxes, frustrations and mysteries of the human condition as Job and Ecclesiastes do. Ultimately, wise men and women follow the star that leads to Jesus 'in whom are hidden all the treasures of wisdom and knowledge' (see Prov. 8 and Col. 2:3).

Psalmody

Then Psalms invite us to cry out to God in heartbroken petition and heartfelt praise. The psalmists joyfully reflect back to God in song what He has revealed about Himself. Psalmody works emotionally, directing our passion beyond idols to the praise of God's glory. Lament songs provide an outlet for our most angry, anguished and negative feelings, and turn them into prayer.

The Psalm collection is remarkable, not least for the way in which it exemplifies how all Scripture emerges from divine-human interaction. In the Psalms we have human words of devotion originally directed to God. Over time, having been gathered together for liturgical use, they have become part of the canonical Scripture as God's Word directed to us. In this way, God endorses and encourages the various ways in which He is pleased to be worshipped – even complained to – all within the security of the covenant relationship.

Prophecy

Prophecy warns us not to speculate on dates or become crystal-ball gazers. Prophecy urges us to open our eyes to the reality behind the scenes of what is going on around us now. It wants us to see past the headlines to what God has done, is doing and will do (more on this later).

It's important for us to understand that Bible prophecy works imaginatively, opening our eyes to reality and challenging us to be counter-cultural. Today we have come to realise that people are changed not so much by direct moral exhortation as by transformed imagination. I like to think that biblical prophecy anticipated this long ago, and sought, by visionary hyperbole and vivid metaphors, to sneak past our jaded mental defences and to implant the Word.

Apocalyptic

Prophecy takes an even more acute form in what is called 'apocalyptic'. An 'apocalypse' is a form of speech or literature that unveils an alternative scenario of reality. This is evident in the book of Daniel, parts of Isaiah and Jeremiah and, of course, in John's Revelation.

As with prophecy in general, 'apocalyptic literature' is not concerned with predicting the future. It is concerned with *unmasking* the present. It serves to unveil the realities around us for what they really are. In this way it opens up the future not as determined by the short-lived powers-that-be, but by the long-term sovereignty of the Lord of history. This is why apocalyptic literature is best interpreted, not by end-time obsessives, but by front-line sufferers in God's resistance movement. In Chris Wright's words,

> 'The Old Testament... is like a great river. There are the different streams of tradition, law, narrative,

poetry, prophecy, wisdom… But in the end they all combine into a single current, flowing deep and strong – the ongoing, irresistible promise of God.'*

Pay attention to the literary form in which a particular Scripture is couched. Ask: What truth is it intended to convey? What effect was it meant to achieve?

*Chris Wright, *Knowing Jesus through the Old Testament: Rediscovering the roots of our faith* (Basingstoke: Marshall Pickering, 1992), p101.

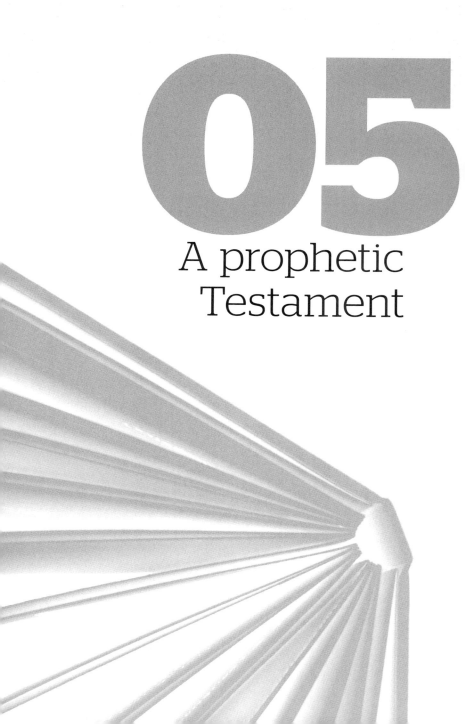

05

A prophetic
Testament

It is worth knowing that the Old Testament as a whole is prophetic.

'Long ago... God spoke to our fathers **by the prophets***'* (Heb. 1:1)

When the author of Hebrews writes that God 'spoke through the prophets', he almost certainly means to include all those through whom God spoke in the first phase of His self-revelation: from Moses, Joshua, David through to the classical prophets.

To say this is to broaden the role played by prophecy in the Old Testament story. Biblical prophecy – even from those overtly said to be 'prophets' – was not primarily concerned with future-telling. Their approach was more subtle and more immediate. They spoke God's Word in the present moment, so as to enable God's people to live faithfully in the light of their God-shaped past and God's promised future.

In particular, prophets deal in *perception*, not prediction. Prophetic speaking and writing aims to open up the eyes of the heart to help us see what we would otherwise miss. It attempts to stir the imagination of its hearers through visions, vivid imagery and poetic pictures. Prophetic speaking and writing offers us a fresh vantage point so that we may look at the world from God's perspective. It helps us to see the present, the past and the future differently.

Prophecy enables us to:
· see the present in a new light
· view the past in fresh perspective
· look at the future with new eyes.

In a new light

First, prophetic vision enables us to *see the present in a new light*.

Busy with work, family and everyday life, just like everyone else, our view of what the real world is can easily shrink to what we interact with. Round-the-clock news confirms that our secular society is determined to press ahead without God. We might become resigned or fearful. We can feel hemmed in, our field of vision limited by the unbelief around us. So it was in ancient Israel. Now, as then, believers need prophets who will offer us an alternative scenario.

It is significant that the two main bursts of Old Testament prophecy occurred at the two main fracture points in Israel's history. The first was prior to the Assyrian attack in the mid-eighth century BC (Amos, Isaiah 1–39), which saw the end of the northern kingdom, Israel. The second took place up to, during and after the final traumatic Babylonian Exile in the sixth century BC. Biblical prophecy is clearly not meant for comfortable speculation but for crises of faith.

Prophets enable us to see past the prevailing imperial propaganda, cultural ideology or spiritual complacency, and they pull out all the stops to do this. They paint vivid pictures, share extravagant visions, enact strange rituals, re-tell the ancient stories in innovative ways... anything to get God's people to see through and beyond things as they are. Prophets want God's people to see deeper into *God's* heart. They strive to re-awaken faith in God's age-old commitments, and to stir trust in God's sovereign agenda. 'Look beyond the obvious,' they plead. 'You may be able to trace God's providential workings and see further even in short-sighted times.'

A fresh perspective

Secondly, prophetic speaking and writing enable us to *view the past in fresh perspective.*

Biblical history can truly be described as 'prophetic history'. Intriguingly, the Jewish canon lists the whole history from Joshua through to 2 Chronicles as 'the former prophets'. It was a prophet's role, even when writing history, to interpret the ways of God to His people. 'Look back over all that has happened to you,' the prophet says. 'Don't you see the footprints of God everywhere? Can't you detect the fingerprints of God all over your history?'

We need then to read the Old Testament narratives as they were intended to be read – prophetically. Viewed this way, we see that biblical history is both theological and redemptive. It recounts a story God is telling in Scripture about what He is planning and doing. Human characters and events become significant for biblical historians, therefore, by being related to and involved with what God is perceived to be doing in working out His saving purposes through human history.

Behind the scenes – behind events described by contemporaries in terms of economics and international politics – can you discern a divine purpose expressed in terms of the judgment and mercy of God?

Speaking truth to power

The emergence of the monarchy in Israel marks a significant change in the role of a prophet. 1 Samuel 9:9 interrupts the narrative to mark that change:

> *'Formerly in Israel, when a man went to enquire of God, he said, "Come, let us go to the seer", for today's "prophet" was formerly called a seer.'*

Why is this significant? Because from now on, the prophets, often resident at court, would be the 'guardians of the theocracy'; upholders of the rule of God over His people. They proved to be thorns in the side of the kings of Israel and Judah, holding them to account for failing to keep covenant with God or lead the people in covenantal ways. To do this, they had to do battle with those they denounced as 'false prophets' – ancient spin-doctors who told the king what he wanted to hear. 'Thus says the Lord' trumps 'thus says the king'.

When Jeremiah receives a word from the Lord for Jehoiakim, he dictates it to Baruch, his scribe and assistant. The king is so affronted when it is read to him that he cuts up the scroll and burns it. Since nothing can stop God's Word, Jeremiah produces a new expanded version of His message so that the king gets more than he bargained for! The crucial point to notice is that God's Word makes as much impact when it is *written and read aloud* as it would have made if spoken directly by the prophet (Jer. 36).

It is worth noting that 1 and 2 Kings can largely be seen as the story of how kingship interacted with the prophets God sent to Israel. How fascinating that the prophets were often court officials and were habitually invading the king's space with the Word of God. Elijah, Elisha, and later Isaiah, exemplify this (see 1 Kings 17–19; 2 Kings 1–3; 19), as do a series of less well-known voices from Abijah (1 Kings 11:29) through to Huldah, who was the major female prophet (2 Kings 22:14–20).

At every turn, throughout the centuries-long decline that eventually brought kingship to an end and sent God's people into exile in Babylon, it is faithfulness to the covenant and not secular success that is the yardstick by which the kings of Israel and Judah are measured. The long rule of Omri is told in six verses because 'he did evil in God's sight' (1 Kings 16:23–28). Josiah merits two chapters because he instituted covenant renewal (2 Kings 22–23).

1 and 2 Chronicles is also history told in a 'prophetic key'. In Chronicles there are a dozen original prophetic speeches not found anywhere else in the Old Testament. The chronicler is concerned to present Israel's history in a certain light and for a particular prophetic purpose. He airbrushes the story of David told in the books of Samuel – not because he wants to mislead, but because he is convinced that God's future for His people was guaranteed in the past by God's personal covenant commitment to David and to his lineage.

Even the writer of Kings, peering through the dark storm clouds engulfing the nation, saw God promising to David 'a lamp that will not go out' (1 Kings 11:36; 15:4; 2 Kings 8:19).

A new hope

Thirdly, prophetic speaking and writing enable us to look to the future through fresh eyes and with new hope.

Contrary to much popular teaching, the classic Old Testament prophets did not offer detailed proof-texts, predicting future events that could be ticked off a list as and when they occurred. They painted in large shapes and bright colours, and undoubtedly spoke more than they themselves knew – as the apostle Peter recognised:

> 'Concerning this salvation, the prophets who prophesied about the grace that was to be yours searched and enquired carefully, enquiring what person or time the Spirit of Christ in them was indicating when he predicted the sufferings of Christ and the subsequent glories.' (1 Pet. 1:10–11)

Whatever the precise shape of this future salvation, the classical prophets like Isaiah were sure that it would involve God doing a 'new thing' (see Isa. 42:9).

Gripped by this vision, the great prophets at the time of the Exile heralded a new exodus, a new kind of shepherd-king, the raising up from spiritual death a new covenant people of God, and even more amazingly, the prospect of God renewing His entire creation. Suffice to say, God's new thing would outdo anything seen before:

> *'Remember not the former things,*
> *nor consider the things of old.*
> *Behold, I am doing a new thing;*
> *now it springs forth, do you not perceive it?'* (Isa. 43:18–19)

Good memories would be eclipsed by even better ones.

Momentum

The Old Testament as a whole is prophetic in that it has an in-built momentum that drives the story forward towards God's intended goal. It is a promise-driven story.

The chronicler, in prophetic mood, searches the sad 800-year-old history of covenant unfaithfulness as though panhandling for gold. He finds in the covenant promise God made to David reassurance that, though the redemptive story has stalled, it has not stopped. By the way he chronicles the past, he aims to stimulate the post-exilic generation to fresh hope and diligence.

The classical prophets constantly recall God's people to their original covenantal vocation. They rebuke complacency, and declare judgment on the rebellion that stands in the way of God's saving plans. They urge God's people to keep track of God's story and to stay in step with it. Prophets speak and act to remove roads-blocks of unbelief from the pathway to future salvation. They seek to move the story on by urging each generation to live in the light of the up-coming 'Day of the Lord' and so to maintain the momentum of God's promise.

Mystery

Much as the Old Testament holds the keys for interpreting the coming of Christ, it nevertheless conceals as well as reveals God's saving purpose. There is in the prophetic Scriptures a mysterious hiddenness as if the saving secret has been hinted at and alluded to, but awaits full disclosure (see Dan. 2:19–22). Paul certainly saw it this way (Rom. 16:25–27; Eph. 3:1–10).

The hiddenness of the secret has led some to speak of the gradual disappearance of God as the Old Testament story draws to its close. In the early stages of the story, miracles abound; seas part, axe-heads float. But the dramatic supernatural intrusions of God so evident in the earlier parts of the story seem to tail off later on. In the book of Esther, for example, God is not mentioned at all, though His providential oversight is surely at work in and through this remarkably shrewd and courageous woman of faith. We might even surmise that if there is any gradual withdrawal of God's overt interventionism, then it may be for a purpose.

Coupled with the way in which the prophets more and more embody and enact the message they are given, this supposed disappearance of God may itself be a way of saying: 'Don't close the book: you haven't seen anything yet.' It is almost as if the way the story ends leaves a vacuum that only incarnation can fill! If so, it is a purpose-driven hiddenness.

There is yet more light and truth to break forth from God's holy Word in the Old Testament Scriptures. Only in the good news of Jesus do we see and hear it. The 'mystery' will turn out to be the 'open secret', now proclaimed in the gospel, that the kingdom-rule of God is paradoxically re-established on earth as it is in heaven through the suffering, death and resurrection of Jesus (Mark 4:11).

Motivation

The momentum maintained through the prophetic word and in the Old Testament as a whole is due to the empowering activity of the Holy Spirit. The Holy Spirit motivates the prophets and inspires their words:

> 'And we have something more sure, the prophetic word, to which you will do well to pay attention as to a lamp shining in a dark place, until the day dawns and the morning star rises in your hearts, knowing this first of all, that no prophecy of Scripture comes from someone's own interpretation. For no prophecy was ever produced by the will of man, but men spoke from God as they were carried along by the Holy Spirit.' (2 Pet. 1:19–21)

Here is another reason why such Spirit-inspired prophetic Scriptures speak powerfully to us. The Holy Spirit reaches back into the Scriptures He originally inspired, and speaks them again in the present tense as if they were intended for us. The Holy Spirit contemporises the old texts:

> 'Therefore, as the Holy Spirit says,
> "Today, if you hear his voice,
> do not harden your hearts as in the rebellion,
> on the day of testing in the wilderness"' (Heb. 3:7–8)

Living as we are on this side of history, we hear the ancient text of Psalm 95 speaking to us as it did to pilgrims at an earlier stage of the faith journey, urging us to hear and believe and obey in our 'today'. David, the author of Psalm 95, is reckoned to have spoken prophetically, his inspired words resonating down the centuries into another day for the people of God (see Acts 2:29–31).

It is the Holy Spirit who energises the inspired text of Scripture so that it is declared and preached as a powerful prophetic word for the present:

'All Scripture is breathed out by God and profitable for teaching, for reproof, for correction, and for training in righteousness' (2 Tim. 3:16).

Every scripture is *God-breathed* – which seems to imply that the very words carry God's stamp, and are freighted with the power of God's own breath or Spirit. In linking this to the incarnation of the Word in Jesus, the letter to the Hebrews therefore has a dynamic and Trinitarian view of the Old Testament Scriptures:

• What God says, Scripture says (Heb. 1:6)
• What Scripture says, the Son says (Heb. 2:11–13; 10:5)
• What Scripture says, the Spirit says (Heb. 3:7; 10:15–17)

John Walton said that 'all the literature of the Old Testament can be considered prophetic literature since it finds its source in God'.[*] What further incentive do we need to listen to these ancient texts and to hear the voice of the living God speaking to us *today* through them?

There's no future in ignoring the past. History matters.

[*]John Walton and D. Brent Sandy, *The Lost World of Scripture: Ancient Literary Culture and Biblical Authority* (Downers Grove, IL, USA: IVP Academic, 2013), p224.

Timeline

Abraham		David
1800 BC		1000 BC

Exodus
1200 BC
From slavery in Egypt

Five stages of Israel's history following the timeline above:

A pilgrim people;
a tribal family

A liberated
people/
the theocratic
nation

The twin 'poles' around which the whole Old Testament

Jesus

Northern
Kingdom
ISRAEL

Southern
Kingdom
JUDAH

Exile

606–520 BC
To slavery in Babylon

An institutional state under monarchy	An afflicted remnant (Exile)	A religious community (post-exilic)

story of Israel revolves are the Exodus and the Exile.

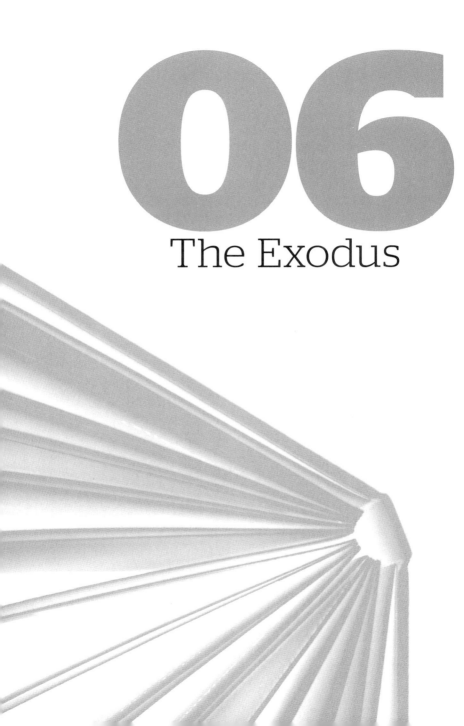

06

The Exodus

It is worth knowing that the Exodus is the effective beginning of the story told in the Old Testament.

Exodus from Egypt. The Great Escape from slavery.

It started with a burning bush and the call of Moses.

A voice from the fire disclosing God's personal covenant name: Yahweh ('I will be what I will be'), usually translated as 'LORD' in upper-case letters.

Next: conflict with Pharaoh and the gods of Egypt.

Impressive plagues on an oppressive regime.

Passover – saved by the blood of a lamb.

Finally, Red Sea parting.

Sinai, smoke on the mountain.

A voice from the fire.

'Ten words' to keep a redeemed people free.

And God makes a covenant with the Israelites.

All these dramatic things define *who Israel is* and what her *role in the world* is to be: a chosen nation for the sake of the unchosen. A royal priesthood to be a means of grace between God and His world. A holy nation to recover the original human calling to be image-bearers of God's character to creation. 'Be holy as I am holy' becomes, throughout Leviticus, Israel's designer label.

Priestly roles, sacrificial rites and complex rules of holiness, remote as they might seem to us, were all intended to maintain Israel's God-glorifying distinctiveness. As the ransomed of the

Lord, Israel was called to show the world that to be redeemed is to come into the fullness of our intended value.

> **Last things first...**
> The Exodus effectively launches the Old Testament's story. Arguably, then, for this reason it is the book of Exodus, not Genesis, which might be seen as the first book of the Bible. What is revealed in Genesis – about God, creation and humankind – was first given to Israel.

And it was in Israel that this revelation was cherished and preserved. In other words, Genesis is best viewed from the standpoint of the events recorded in Exodus. From this perspective what we find in Genesis are answers to the kind of questions that would inevitably have arisen among these uniquely elected former slaves. At least three questions spring to mind:

1. How did we get into Egypt in the first place, and why were we liberated?

Genesis 12–50 provides the answer. The immediate pretext for the Exodus is the story of Joseph, which explains why Abraham's descendants ended up in Egypt and defiantly assert that 'God meant it for good' (see Gen. 37–50 for the whole story).

Beyond this stands God's original promise and covenant commitment to Abraham (Gen. 12;15). This foundational promise, reaffirmed to Isaac (Gen. 26:3–5), and to Jacob (Gen. 28:13–14), connects the patriarchal stories, and shapes the course of history as far as Jesus (Gal. 3:7–14).

2. Why were we, Israel, exclusively chosen by God?

Genesis 1–11 is placed there to answer this question. Israel exists and is chosen *for the sake of the whole world*.

Noah (portrayed in the old stories as a 'new Adam'), together with his family, is preserved by God at the flood as the down-payment on humanity's future, set on an earth guaranteed by covenant until God's redemptive work is finished.

Abraham is later called from the world of nations (Gen. 10) to be the means of God blessing all nations (Gen. 12:3). He is called from the city that mankind is building (Heb. 11:5) to move in faith towards the city God is building (Heb. 11:10).

The people of Israel inherit this destiny which touches the whole world, even the entire created order. Israel, in effect, is called to become the sample new human race heading for the Promised Land – and the Promised Land is the microcosm of the renewed earth God has set His eyes on. This is Israel's key role in God's strategic plan of salvation. One nation for all nations:

'My treasured possession among all peoples, for all the earth is mine' (Exod. 19:5)

So Genesis 1–11, in setting the scene for Abraham, sets Israel on a world stage with a world mission. And this then answers the big question…

3. Who is this God?

Above all else, the text of Genesis 12–50 highlights the amazing grace of God in working out His purpose through the emotional resistance and even moral failures of His chosen partners in the venture. These human frailties are realistically noted but do nothing to obscure the faithfulness of a promise-making, covenant-keeping God.

Genesis is not primarily interested (and nor should we be) in parading the patriarchs as spiritual or ethical models, but as reluctant heroes plucked from domestic obscurity to be key players in God's bigger story. The same is true for Israel as a nation (see Deut. 7:7–9). Genesis 1–11 encapsulates Israel's joyous discovery that the God who has redeemed them and covenanted with them at Sinai is no mere tribal, or ethnic or even national god, but is in fact *the one creator God* of the whole world!

It is well worth noting that the book of Exodus emphasises that it is God's grace that initiates redemption and covenant relationship; it is a mistake to offset a gracious New Testament against a legalistic Old Testament. As Exodus 1–18 demonstrates, Israel's life was founded on grace and redemption. God's love is *compassionate* in that He responds to the current plight of the children of Israel, and God's love is *covenantal* in remembering his long-standing commitments to the patriarchs. 'God heard their groaning and remembered his covenant with Abraham, Isaac and Jacob' (see Exod. 2:24).

God tells Moses His personal, covenant name. Rescue and redemption and covenant-making follow. The blood of the lamb – which saves the Israelite households – is forever commemorated in the Passover feast and re-enacted in the ongoing animal sacrifices. The groan of slavery becomes the cry of freedom. Israel sings the song of a people who believe they will not be slaves again (see Exod. 15:1–18).

So why the law?

The law (Torah) was not given so that Israel could earn salvation by good works. The law was given to a people already redeemed as the description of how a covenant people should live. It is intended to be a 'law of liberty'. It seeks to promote a free, just, caring society, which is the opposite of the slave-driven, oppressive and unjust society Israel suffered under while in Egypt. David Gill rightly calls the Ten Commandments the 'menu of the feast of freedom'.*

'Redemption' language implies being bought at a price and so being owned or possessed by another. Freedom is God's gift, enjoyed in relationship with Him. This is so counter-cultural to the self-determined, freedom-of-choice way of life so celebrated in the consumerist world. But indeed it is real freedom: from oppression, into the service of God.

For this reason, Israel is called God's 'son': 'Let my firstborn son go free' (Exod. 4:22–23). This designation will one day devolve onto her king (see 2 Sam. 7:14) and will eventually mark out Jesus as the royal Son who lives out Israel's calling (Matt. 3:17; 4:3), succeeding in the test where nation and kings have failed. The 'way of the Lord' that John the Baptist prepares will lead Jesus to the cross, which will prove to be the new exodus the world needs (Luke 9:31).

Salvation is to be freed from sin and self to serve God.

*David W. Gill, *Becoming Good: Building Moral Character* (Downers Grove, IL, USA: IVP, 2000) p156.

07
The Exile

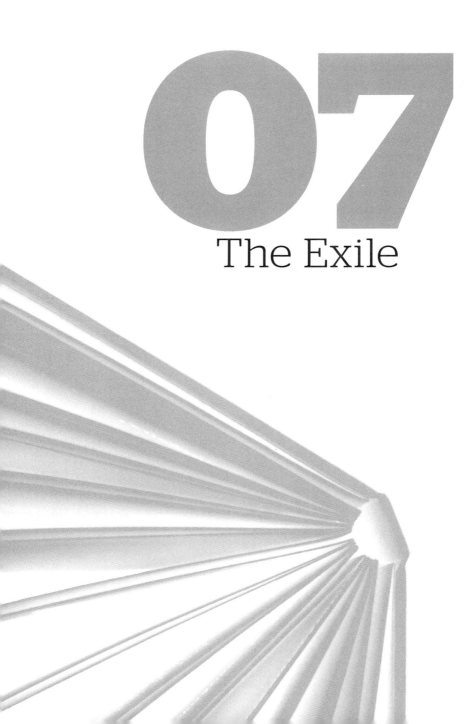

It is worth knowing that the Babylonian Exile effectively 'ends' the Old Testament story and shapes the future of God's people and God's plan.

Exile.

In a word: pain. Loss of home. Deportation to a foreign land. An uncertain future. Even more devastating for the exiles from Judah – the holy Temple desecrated. The holy city, Jerusalem, in ruins. All the outward symbols of national identity gone.

The Babylonian invasion of Judah and the exiling of its leading citizens felt like the death of God's chosen people. And perhaps the death of God, too.

How ironic for this special people; to have once come from one form of slavery and, at the last, to end up in another. How poignant that this should be in Babylonia, which Abraham had left more than a thousand years earlier! To lose the Promised Land was to fall under the ultimate curse on covenant unfaithfulness: 'And you shall be plucked off the land' (Deut. 8:63; 29:27–28).

Grief was the first reaction – overwhelming grief. Singers and poets and prophets strained to give expression to it.

'By the waters of Babylon,
There we sat down and wept,
when we remembered Zion.
On the willows there
we hung up our lyres.
For there our captors

required of us songs,
and our tormentors, mirth, saying,
"Sing us one of the songs of Zion!"
How shall we sing the LORD's song
in a foreign land?' (Psa. 137:1–4)

As if trying to contain the pain, the trauma is channelled into the five poems of the aptly-named book of Lamentations, the most tear-stained book in the Old Testament.

Jeremiah

The prophet Jeremiah had bravely warned of the impending catastrophe. He was bitterly opposed for advocating that people submit to the Babylonian invasion, as God's judgment upon them. Later, he again went against popular opinion, telling the exiles not to hope for a quick return, but to *settle in* for the long-haul. Exile would last some 70 years, he announces.

In his famous letter, he urges them to seek the peace and prosperity of the pagan city, indeed to pray for it, in order that they might prosper with it! Trust God, the prophet pleads. Your covenant-keeping God has 'plans to give you a future and a hope' (Jer. 29:11).

Finally, Jeremiah offers hope beyond exile in the wonderful *promise* of a new covenant in which God would work to change His people from the inside out, creating a truly faithful covenant community (Jer. 31:31–34).

Ezekiel

Ezekiel, a young trainee priest, was himself a deportee to Babylon around 606 BC, sharing exile in solidarity with the people. There, in a vision, the Spirit showed him God's glory tragically leaving the defiled Temple in Jerusalem. But God's *absence* from the Temple is matched by a remarkable *reassurance*. Ezekiel sees in a vision the glory of God arriving on God's mobile chariot-throne, right there on the banks of the canal in Babylon where the exiled community was settled. God was not dead but alive – not absent but gloriously present with His people right there in exile!

The prophets of the Exile made it clear that not only the people but the *kings* had failed. With the demise of Judah's last king, both Jeremiah and Ezekiel looked forward to the day when God Himself would redeem the role of king, as the ideal shepherd of His people (see Jer. 23 and Ezek. 34). Tantalisingly, Ezekiel is unsure whether God will send a Davidic prince or come *in person* to do the job of bringing His kingdom in.

Later still, Ezekiel prophesies – as Jeremiah does – that God will replace the hard hearts of His rebellious people with soft, responsive hearts. This spiritual heart transplant will create *a new covenant people* (Ezek. 36). God's own creative Spirit will raise His 'dead' people to life again in an act of 'resurrection' (Ezek. 37)!

Isaiah

It is left to Isaiah to envision what salvation might look like on the other side of exile. Isaiah gathers up all these previous strands of prophecy into a wonderful message of good news (Isa. 40:9). God will return to His people to take up His rightful place as the centre of His people's lives once again (Isa. 40:3). God will forgive His sinful people and lead them out in a 'new exodus', which eclipses the original deliverance from Egypt (Isa. 43; 44). God will bring in His *kingly rule* of peace and salvation (Isa. 52:7) through the obedient suffering and sacrificial death of a mysterious servant-king (Isa. 42; 53). And beyond the immediate horizon – the vision of a *new creation* (Isa. 65; 66).

Hope for the future?

Exile concentrated minds wonderfully. It prompted a serious re-assessment of the past, and of the prospects for the future – and this is what we have in 1 and 2 Kings, and 1 and 2 Chronicles. As we saw earlier, each answers a slightly different question. 1 and 2 Kings seeks to answer the question: 'Why did we end up in exile?', while 1 and 2 Chronicles asks: 'Is there any hope for the future?'

Indeed, exile was almost certainly the catalyst for the formation of the canon of Scripture. One can imagine seriously penitent people saying to one another in exile and in the aftermath of exile, 'Where did we go wrong? What did the prophets say of whom we took so little notice? Has anyone kept records of their prophecies? Can anyone recall those ancient stories about the patriarchs and about creation? They surely tell us who we are and why we are here. They surely remind us who our God is and how much he has invested in us, in our survival and in our future.'

The recovery of God's Word had given hope once before when the high priest, Hilkiah, had found the book of the law in the Temple, seemingly out of sight and mind. Its rediscovery prompted a genuine renewal under King Josiah (1 Kings 22–23). Now, post-exile, with the loss of the Temple, the sacred texts became even more important. Ezra, like a new Moses, recalls the people to close attention and adherence to the Word of God.

It is in the post-exilic period that the first moves are made to collect the old stories and sagas and prophecies and to begin to arrange them into a cohesive scriptural canon. Deuteronomy can now be read in a fresh way in the light of its warnings coming true. So the post-exilic editors add a footnote to the old text: 'as it is this day' (Deut. 29:28).

Scripture feels now like a living voice from God for anyone who has lived through or in the aftermath of such terrible events. What an encouragement the ancient texts were! Imagine enduring Babylonian overlordship, or being back in the Promised Land but under Persian rule, and rejoicing as the Torah took its final scriptural form. Imagine the new hope aroused by feeling the force of Genesis 1 as it counters rival Ancient Near Eastern versions of the world's origins, and as it sharpens your sense of identity as the special people of the one true God in a pagan culture.

Exile remains a recurring motif for the people back in the land as the restoration begins, prompted by the prophets Haggai and Zechariah. Exile is not really over while God's people remain under pagan domination. 'Behold, we are slaves to this day; in the land that you gave to our fathers' (Neh. 9:36; see also Ezra 9:6–9). Neither the undiminished reality of exile nor the unsatisfied longing for new covenant salvation were resolved in the post-exilic restored community, even under Ezra and Nehemiah.

The sense of being somehow *still in exile* eventually becomes the matrix that best explains the ministry and mission of Jesus, as the openings of each of the four Gospels show.

> In exploring the saving implications of the gospel, the apostle Paul follows the sequence of salvation outlined by the exilic prophets: new exodus, with a new covenant people under new Kingship, entering the new creation, which will one day affect the whole earth. (See 2 Cor. 1–9 and Rom. 5–8.)

For the four Gospel writers, this *end of exile* mood is the backdrop for the coming of Jesus and the best window through which to grasp His significance. They all link Isaiah's voice crying in the wilderness, announcing that exile is finally over (Isa. 40), to the ministry of John the Baptist as he seeks to prepare Israel for the coming of God's kingdom through Jesus.

So Jesus proclaims the end of 'exile' by offering forgiveness and announcing that God's kingdom rule is at work again. He obliquely refers to Himself as Isaiah's suffering servant, the mysterious agent of salvation, but baffles His hearers by linking to it the triumph and glory of Daniel's 'Son of Man'.

In the shadow of death, Jesus establishes the new covenant, promised by Jeremiah, through His own blood. He goes to the cross to bear the 'curse' of exile (Deut. 29:25–28) in place of God's rebellious people. And the 'death' and 'resurrection' of God's people – envisaged by Ezekiel as the means by which ultimate salvation will come – is something Jesus enacts 'solo', not as a mere figure of speech but as a boundary-breaking reality.

The release of the Spirit at Pentecost (as described in Acts 2) is therefore to be viewed not so much as the birth of the Church, but rather as the renewal of Israel as the new covenant people of God. To this forgiven, cleansed, Spirit-filled people – according to the exilic prophets' perspective – God would rapidly add the Gentiles who repent and believe.

Return from exile prefigures the homecoming of all who respond to the gospel invitation to be reconciled with God.

08

Moving towards Jesus

It is worth knowing that the Old Testament moves towards its climax in Jesus Christ.

'**in these last days** he has spoken to us **by his Son**'
(Heb. 1:2)

In the days of my childhood, there were two editions of the local newspaper – one at midday, and an updated version in the early evening. At lunchtime, on a board outside the newsagents, these words would appear under the main headline: *Full story in the final edition.* This could be written at any point of the Old Testament Scriptures.

There is a Christ-intended trajectory in the Old Testament. All the previous and partial revelation becomes the full and final edition of the story now updated in Him. The provisional has come to its appointed time. The promises now reach their moment of fulfilment. The progressive and cumulative unfolding of the first phase of revelation peaks here. The prophetic momentum of the Old Testament has carried God's truth to its intended destination: God's Son. God's full story awaits the final edition: Jesus.

> 'Whatever has been promised by God gets stamped with the Yes of Jesus' (2 Cor. 1:20, *The Message*).
> He is the goal (the 'telos') of the law (Rom. 10:4).

The reason for this is that in the coming of God's Son, the 'last days' have dawned. Contrary to some popular prophecy and end-times teaching, we have been in the 'last days' since the Day of Pentecost, when Joel's prophecy began to find its fulfilment (see Acts 2:16–17).

In Jesus, 'the age to come' (as the author of Hebrews calls it) has already broken into what Paul calls 'the present evil age' (Gal. 1:4; Heb. 6:5). Here is continuity: the same God speaking. But here is discontinuity: the complete picture now contrasted with a partial one.

In chart form, our life *now*, between the times, looks like this:

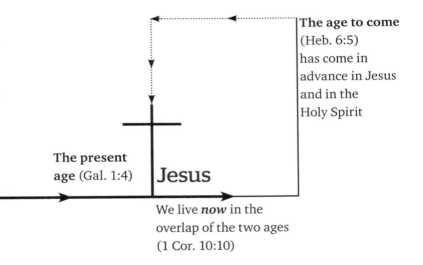

The age to come (Heb. 6:5) has come in advance in Jesus and in the Holy Spirit

The present age (Gal. 1:4)

Jesus

We live *now* in the overlap of the two ages (1 Cor. 10:10)

By His Son...

God has now spoken fully and finally because he has spoken 'by his Son'. The Son of God is the eternal 'Word of God' made flesh among us as Jesus, full of grace and truth, glorious to behold (John 1:14–16). And the author of Hebrews agrees! All God has to say – His first and final word – is Jesus...

*'whom he appointed the heir of all things, through
whom also he created the world. He is the radiance of
the glory of God and the exact imprint of his nature,
and he upholds the universe by the word of his power.'*
(Heb. 1:2–3)

Who better to sum up God's revelation of Himself than the one
whom God appointed the heir of all things, through whom also
He created the world? No one knows better than God's Son why
the creator God made the world or what its intended future is.

No one else reveals God like God's Son, because He has
insider-knowledge of the Trinity; He radiates out to us the
inner glory that is uniquely God's. He has the 'exact imprint
of God's nature' stamped uniquely on His human nature. He
has come to fulfil the earlier longings, evoked in the psalmist
by God's Spirit, for a future day of salvation (Heb. 10:5–10).

The Son is illuminated by the brilliant light coming from
God's future and a shadow is cast backwards into what we
call the Old Testament era. Now, in the Son, the shadow has
become substantial reality (see Heb. 10:1).

Promise and fulfilment

If we look for a great creative mind who first made these crucial
connections between promise and fulfilment in Jesus, surely
we need look no further than Jesus Himself. It was Jesus who
joined up the 'prophetic dots' in an unprecedented way. The
Gospel writers assure us it was Jesus who inspired this reading
of the Old Testament. Jesus challenges the Pharisees as keen
Bible students over their interpretation of it:

*'You search the Scriptures because you think that in them
you have eternal life; and it is they that* **bear witness**

about me, *yet you refuse to come to me that you may have life.'* (John 5:39–40, emphasis added)

On the road to Emmaus, the two disconsolate disciples experience both soul-stirring rebuke and heart-warming hope as Jesus opens the Scriptures to them:

> *'And beginning with Moses and all the Prophets, he interpreted to them in all the Scriptures the things concerning himself... And their eyes were opened, and they recognized him. And he vanished from their sight. They said to each other, "Did not our hearts burn within us while he talked to us on the road, while he opened to us the Scriptures?"'* (Luke 24:27,31–32)

Later in the Upper Room, Jesus says to His gathered disciples:

> *'"These are my words that I spoke to you while I was still with you, that everything written about me in the Law of Moses and the Prophets and the Psalms must be fulfilled." Then he opened their minds to understand the Scriptures.'* (Luke 24:44–45)

At this point, it is important to guard against a common misconception. Jesus is *not* saying that scattered proof-texts or isolated predictions land on-target in Him. He is claiming much more than that. Significantly, Jesus refers to the 'The Law, the Prophets, and the Psalms' as being fulfilled by and in Him. These three terms cover the entire Old Testament Scriptures. They show that by the time of Jesus, the Jewish canon of Scripture had already in principle been formalised and described in this threefold way. And Jesus knew of it.

What Jesus is claiming, then, is that the whole previous

phase of the story is now being successfully gathered up in Him. All those vivid Bible stories are really part of one grand story: the story of God's redemptive plan for His people and His creation. All the laws, songs, prophecies and words of wisdom are brought to a saving climax in Him as He recapitulates the story and sings the song, embodying God's Word and wisdom in their fullest expression.

Jesus' interaction with Old Testament Scripture

1. Jesus can be explained only by tracing His roots in the covenant story of Israel told in Scripture.

Matthew tells us this by opening his account of the story of Jesus with a genealogy. He makes Jesus the conclusive chapter in a story stretching back to the Babylonian Exile, then further back to David, and beyond that to Abraham who is called to be the means of grace and blessing to the world (Matt. 1:1–17; 28:18–20).

2. Jesus shapes His life and vocation by Scripture (Heb. 10:5–10).

Jesus resists temptation where Israel had not, by holding fast to what is written in God's Word (Matt. 4:1–7; citing Deut. 8:3; 6:16 and Psa. 91:11–12).

3. Jesus specifically endorses the Old Testament and claims to fulfil it.

> 'Do not think that I have come to abolish the Law or the Prophets; I have not come to abolish them but to **fulfil** them.' (Matt. 5:17, emphasis added)

Jesus both intensifies what was said before (Matt. 5:22) and has God's authority uniquely to qualify, amend and expand on it.

Of course, looking at the Old Testament through the lens of Jesus makes many things clearer. It puts much that went before into true perspective. But of one thing we can be sure: when Jesus says of Scripture, 'But I say to you…' He is not contradicting the God who spoke before, but fulfilling the Father's will and intention.

Without the Old Testament Scriptures we can never hope to understand Jesus. Equally, without Jesus, we will never fully understand the Old Testament.

09

The significance
of salvation

It is worth knowing that the Old Testament provides patterns that illuminate the significance of salvation in Christ.

*'In these last days he has spoken to us by his Son… having become as much **superior to angels** as the name he has inherited is **more excellent** than theirs.'* (Heb. 1:2–4)

Like the author of Hebrews, Paul compares earlier events with fulfilment in Christ when he warns the Corinthians not to repeat the same mistakes made by the Israelites in the wilderness wanderings after the Exodus:

'Now these things took place as examples for us, that we might not desire evil as they did… Now these things happened to them as an example, but they were written down for our instruction, on whom the end of the ages has come.' (1 Cor. 10:6,11)

The kind of comparison Paul makes here is called 'typology' after the Greek word *tupos* – used twice in the text above, and translated as 'example'. It is an important key to biblical interpretation. Typology is a way of noting the correspondence between events or stages of the same God working in an earlier stage of history with what He does later.

This way of reading Scripture confirms our faith by showing that God's wise sovereignty providentially superintends the entire history, even if it soon becomes apparent that what comes later exceeds and eclipses what came earlier.

> There is *continuity*. One God speaking; one story. This means that what God does in one era can be compared or contrasted with what He does at a later time.
>
> But the 'last days' mark a *discontinuity* as well. The revelation that 'in these last days he has spoken to us by his Son' creates a dramatic new situation calling for new eyes and ears. It soon becomes apparent that what comes later exceeds and eclipses what came earlier. What comes later is an escalation or advance on the earlier stage.

How does typology work?

1. It highlights the superiority of Jesus.
Once again, we can look to the letter to the Hebrews for this:

> 'After making purification for sins, he sat down at the right hand of the Majesty on high, having become as much superior to angels as the name he has inherited is more excellent than theirs.' (Heb. 1:3–4)

In the Scriptures, angels are 'ministering spirits', but Jesus has a superior rank and name to them. Moses was a faithful servant, but Jesus is superior and His revelation is definitive because He is more than a servant in God's house; He is a Son *over* God's house (Heb. 3:1–6). Similarly, He eclipses His namesake, Joshua, by leading believers not just to the 'rest' of the promised land of Canaan but to the 'rest' of God's eternal kingdom (Heb. 2:10; 4:8–9). In His sacrificial death, Jesus shows Himself superior to Aaron and the Levitical priests by offering *Himself* as the atoning victim, and by ushering His sanctified sinners into the heavenly presence of God.

2. Typological interpretation works on a large scale.

The biblical version of the human story is a larger scale version of the story of Israel. Creation and covenant are followed by sin, exile and restoration. Israel's covenant failure, which led to expulsion from the Promised Land, is a pattern for the expulsion of Adam and Eve from the Garden of Eden.

Israel's literal exile from the Promised Land represents the spiritual alienation of all humanity from God. Similarly, homecoming from exile serves as a prototype for the infinitely larger reconciliation with God for all people that the gospel offers. Paul describes Adam as 'a *type* of the one who was to come' (Rom. 5:14, emphasis added).

Jesus, Israel's Messiah, appears also as the Last Adam – the truly representative human being. His obedient faithfulness even to death undoes the first Adam's fault and so 'much more' (see Rom. 5:10–21).

3. Large scale comparisons and patterns can enrich our understanding.

It is this typological development of Old Testament themes in the New Testament that enables salvation to be described in expansive terms: new exodus, new covenant, new Davidic kingship, new temple and new creation.

These large-scale comparisons of Old and New Testament events and persons in no way diminish the importance of the Old Testament's witness to truth. Just as Jesus fulfils the earlier patterns, so these patterns – or types – enrich our understanding of who Jesus is and what He has achieved.

At the same time, the comparisons accentuate the fact that the Old Testament needs to be read in the light cast on the past by 'the last days' in which we now live. As we saw before, Paul urges his Corinthian readers to let the downfall of the wilderness wanderers be an 'example' to them, precisely because they are those 'on whom the end of the ages has come' (1 Cor. 10:11). They are in a more privileged place with more expected of them and more to lose, but also with more going for them.

The author of Hebrews makes a similar comparison by his use of the theme of 'rest' (Heb. 3–4). He sees it as having a threefold reference. Glancing *back*, as it were, he sees that the promised resting place for God's pilgrim people in the Promised Land (Heb. 3:18) was prefigured in God's Sabbath rest from His creation work (Heb. 4:4). Looking *forward*, he perceives that the 'rest' of settling in the Promised Land pre-figures the final Sabbath of the rest of faith in the promised kingdom of God, the believer's ultimate homeland. Fulfilment in Christ is already enjoyed by believers in Christ (Heb. 4:3) and yet the kingdom-rest still awaits (Heb. 4:9). Gospel truth oscillates around these three points to impress upon believers the need to remember that they cannot attain this saving rest by their own efforts (Heb. 4:9–11) but, paradoxically, must 'strive to enter that rest' by obedient trust.

The full story in the final edition is not to be missed!

The writer of Hebrews has a distinctive take on this that is worth noting and worth repeating.

Moving from Old Testament to New, from provisional to final revelation, from the 'long-ago' to the 'last days', marks an advance and development. But the move – we repeat – is not from what was bad to what is good, but from what was good to what is *better*. It is this 'better' that is the characteristic note struck by the author of Hebrews.

Jesus exercises a superior priesthood by virtue of His indestructible life: His atonement for sins is based on 'better' sacrifices with blood that 'speaks a better word than the blood of Abel' (Heb. 9:23; 12:24). He is the guarantor of a new and 'better' covenant 'enacted on better promises' made 'long ago' by God to Jeremiah (Jer. 7:22; 8:6).

We are joined to the long march of faith begun by Noah and Abraham (Heb. 11), but 'God had provided something better for us, that apart from us they should not be made perfect' (Heb. 11:40). We have already 'arrived' at Mount Zion (Heb. 12:18) and have already received a kingdom that cannot be shaken. Emboldened, we march on to the 'better country' and the city with 'foundations whose designer and builder is God'.

To summarise, Jesus said to them, 'Therefore every scribe who has been trained for the kingdom of heaven is like a master of a house, who brings out of his treasure what is new and what is old' (Matt. 13:52). The new revelation is not added to the old; nor does the new replace the old. There is still one revelatory story. But the 'new' interprets and renews the old. The old, stored away as inherited treasure, finds its value enhanced when it is brought out into the light of the new day dawning in Jesus.

Make the connections, trace the trajectories, watch for the scale models of the larger version coming later in the Gospels.

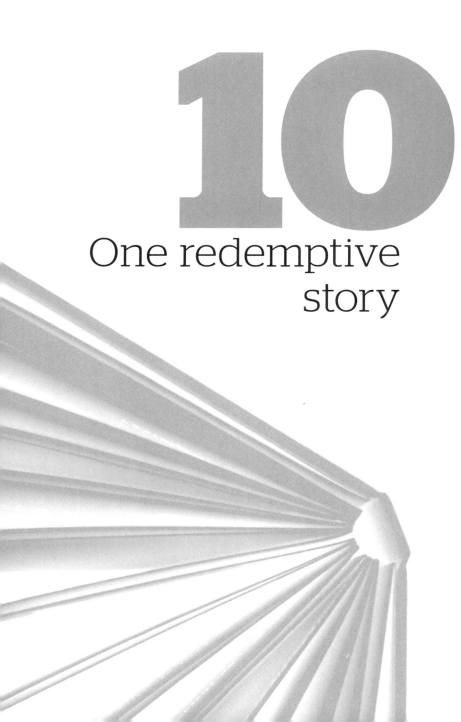

10

One redemptive story

It is worth knowing that the Old Testament tells one overall redemptive story.

> '*in these last days he has spoken to us by his Son, whom he appointed* **the heir of all things, through whom also he created the world**.' (Heb. 1:2)

Missing the wood for the trees is a well-worn cliché for good reason. Seeing the 'wood' as well as the 'trees' is vital for anyone seriously wanting to understand the Bible. We need to keep our eyes on the big picture. The danger is that we 'cut the long story short' by majoring on minor things. By fixating on fascinating smaller episodes, we can fail to appreciate how they connect up as chapters in a larger, longer story. That story ranges from creation ('through whom he created all things') to consummation ('the heir of all things').

What the Old Testament establishes is that there is no more fundamental way of talking about God than in a *story*. Let's not misuse the Bible as if it were a collection of proof-texts to be organised into our own predetermined doctrinal position. Under pressure to 'make the Bible relevant', we can be tempted to trivialise or privatise its overall message, reducing its impact to feel-good slogans. By treating the Bible in this way, we squeeze the life out of it and reduce it to a flat book of moral instruction. If we assume we are reading a moralistic book primarily telling us *what to do*, we may miss the good news of *what God can do*.

The story

The Bible has come to us essentially as a story – a vast, sprawling, untidy, story – but a story nonetheless. Of course, not every part is narrative in form (see Chapter 4). But all the parts have significance only as contributing to or reflecting the grand narrative the Bible unfolds. Eugene Peterson says this:

> 'The way the Bible is written is as important as what is written in it: narrative – this huge, capacious story that pulls us into its plot and shows us our place in its development from beginning to end. It takes the whole Bible to read any part of the Bible.'*

In other words, rambling and muddled and topsy-turvy as this long historical story is, we can detect a movement and purpose that shows God to be its author. And by saying God is the author of this story, we are recognising that the threads of meaning, the covenantal connections and the trajectories of truth are all traceable to His sovereign purpose.

The one creator God initiates this story, and steers it to its intended goal in the face of history's setbacks and rebuffs. In the gripping account of how God achieves this, we discover *what kind of God* this God is. And we come to realise, crucially, that God is not only the author of the story but *the chief actor in the story.* This is to say that God works out His authorial purposes from inside, not outside, the story. God does not exist in some 'Olympian' detachment from the world He has made. Instead He has fully immersed Himself in the history of His creation, willingly making Himself vulnerable to its pain and ambiguity.

By working *within* the drama, as actor as well as author, God exposes Himself to misunderstanding, puts His reputation for holiness and omnipotence on the line, and risks His good name through association with some pretty shady characters. In short, God is willing to become the God of Abraham, Isaac, and even – particularly even – Jacob! Meeting God like this in His own story, we find a God who is involved, intimate, wild, passionate, innovative, utterly faithful, vulnerable, open and persuadable – a tough and tender God who travels and travails with Israel with genuine emotions.

We know that so much of what happens in history – and that includes Old Testament history – occurs by human ingenuity and initiative, whether for good or ill. But God seems able and willing not just to oversee the process, but to work in and through it for His own good purpose. Human beings seem free to decide and act; but God does too. This implies – as the philosophers put it – that God's freedom and our freedom is not a 'zero-sum' game; that is, we do not have to choose either one or the other.

The Old Testament reveals something far subtler and more intriguing. God is not a vague backdrop to a world run on secular or humanistic lines. Without micro-managing the lives of free and responsible human agents, God interacts with the ups and downs of human history so that an underlying and coherent story can be discerned. It is a story that reflects His choosing and doing as He unfolds His saving plan. It is as if God did not think that being God was something to be exploited to His own selfish advantage, but humbled Himself to the level of His human partners, submitting to bear the cost of whatever His creation might come to!

Covenant stages

One helpful way of grasping the coherence of the Old Testament is to notice the covenant commitments God makes at various crucial junctures to move the story on. You can trace its progress through God's covenants with Noah, Abraham, Israel, David, and the new covenant promised by the exilic prophets (as we explored in Chapter 7). It is God's promise to Abraham, later sealed by covenant, that reveals God's saving plans and explains His providential patience as history unfolds:

> 'Now the LORD said to Abram, "Go from your country and your kindred and your father's house to the land that I will show you. And I will make of you a great nation, and I will bless you and make your name great, so that you will be a blessing. I will bless those who bless you, and him who dishonours you I will curse, and in you all the families of the earth shall be blessed."'
> (Gen. 12:1–3)

You can see how this unfolds by reading Galatians 3:7–29.

As we read the Old Testament we can follow the covenantal trail until it leads us to Jesus who is the convergence point of the story. Attentive readers of the covenantal progress of the story soon begin to experience its cumulative force.

Noah recapitulates Adam's story. Israel is entrusted with Adam and Noah's vocation and Abraham's promised destiny. The king in Israel then incorporates the destiny and future of his people. Israel's covenant charter, it is promised, will take the form of a dynamic new covenant outworking through the atoning suffering of a special servant of God and the special gift of God's own Spirit.

Jesus gathers in all these threads, making sense of each one. He faithfully re-runs Israel's story and in doing so successfully re-writes the human story. The story of Jesus is the climax of the long earlier parts of God's story and the key to its unfolding in the future. Remember – without the Old Testament we cannot begin to understand Jesus and without Jesus the Old Testament makes no final sense.

In Jesus all the promises and plans of God converge, the Israel story is conclusively redrawn, the world's story is redeemingly re-written and the story of God is fully revealed.

The Old Testament heroes of faith are rightly celebrated in the roll call of Hebrews 11. Their individual histories with God are gripping and memorable. All of them enjoyed fellowship with God, but are notable not for being paragons of virtue, whether moral or spiritual. What makes them famous is that in their time and place they heeded the call to be part of the ongoing story of God's redemption, which outlives them and finally emerges as the Jesus story. Like a good detective novel, there is a deeper plot beneath the storylines that only surfaces at the end. In its climax in Jesus Christ, it reaches out to include us:

'And all these, though commended through their faith, did not receive what was promised, since God had provided something better for us, that apart from us they should not be made perfect.' (Heb. 11:39–40)

As we immerse ourselves in this big biblical story we encounter the real God, and get to find out what He's really like. Following the narrative flow of God's self-disclosure, we learn to appreciate the satisfying unity of Scripture while enjoying its fascinating diversity. And as we read Scripture we are drawn into the action, finding ourselves caught up in the saving movement of God.

By hearing and performing the text, we learn to indwell the story more and more, looking out on our contemporary world through more biblical eyes. Instead of having to make the Bible relevant to our modern lives, we find that we are being made relevant to the Bible!

> 'For whatever was written in former days was written for our instruction, that through endurance and through the encouragement of the Scriptures we might have hope...
> For I tell you that Christ became a servant to the circumcised to show God's truthfulness, in order to confirm the promises given to the patriarchs, and in order that the Gentiles might glorify God for his mercy. As it is written, "Therefore I will praise you among the Gentiles, and sing to your name."' (Rom. 15:4–9)

Above all, we are encouraged by those Old Testament Scriptures to trust and travel with God, confident that His covenant love will not let us go or let us down.

Read the Old Testament because it tells God's story and our story too.

---

*Eugene Peterson, *Eat This Book: A Conversation in the Art of Spiritual Reading* (Grand Rapids, MI, USA: Eerdmans, 2006), p48.

Further reading

You may find the following helpful in your further study. Most of my suggestions are entry-level books, with exception to those marked with an asterisk, which are more advanced.

On the nature of Scripture:

Paul Helm and Carl Trueman (Eds.), *The Trustworthiness of God: Perspectives on the Nature of Scripture* (Nottingham: Apollos, 2002)*

Jim Packer, *God Has Spoken* (London: Hodder, 1965/2016)*

Jim Packer, *Honouring the Written Word of God: Collected Shorter Writings (Vol. 3)* (Milton Keynes: Paternoster, 1999)*

Timothy Ward, *Words of Life: Scripture as the Living and Active Word of God* (Downers Grove, IL, USA: IVP, 2009)

Paul Wells, *Taking the Bible at its Word* (Tain, Scotland: Christian Focus, 2013)

On how to interpret the Bible (both Testaments):

Gordon Fee and Douglas Stuart, *How to Read the Bible for All Its Worth* (Grand Rapids, MI, USA: Zondervan, 2014)

Gordon Fee and Douglas Stuart, *How to Read the Bible Book by Book* (Grand Rapids, MI, USA: Zondervan, 2002)

John Walton and Brent Sandy, *The Lost World of Scripture: Ancient Literary Culture and Biblical Authority* (Downers Grove, IL, USA: IVP, 2013)*

On the Old Testament specifically:

Tremper Longman, *Making Sense of the Old Testament* (Grand Rapids, MI, USA: Baker, 1998)

Alec Motyer, *A Scenic Route through the Old Testament* (Downers Grove, IL, USA: IVP, 2016)

John Walton, *The Lost World of Genesis One; Ancient Cosmology and the Origins Debate* (Downers Grove, IL, USA: IVP, 2009)

On the storyline of the Bible:

Philip Greenslade, *A Passion for God's Story* (Farnham: CWR, 2006)

Chris Wright, *Knowing Jesus through the Old Testament: Rediscovering the roots of our faith* (Basingstoke: Marshall Pickering, 1992)

On how to hear God's Word:

Eugene Peterson, *Eat This Book: A Conversation in the Art of Spiritual Reading* (Grand Rapids, MI, USA: Eerdmans, 2006)

Also available from Philip Greenslade

10 things worth knowing about
The New Testament

This book will help you engage with the Bible and the story of Jesus. Understand passages in context and appreciate how and why they are God's Word for us today.

Drawing on his 40 years of biblical teaching experience, Philip illuminates ten key aspects from the New Testament.

Available direct from CWR or from a Christian bookshop. Find out more about Philip Greenslade's books and courses at **www.cwr.org.uk**

Courses and seminars

Waverley Abbey College

Publishing and media

Conference facilities

Transforming lives

CWR's vision is to enable people to experience personal transformation through applying God's Word to their lives and relationships.

Our Bible-based training and resources help people around the world to:
• Grow in their walk with God
• Understand and apply Scripture to their lives
• Resource themselves and their church
• Develop pastoral care and counselling skills
• Train for leadership
• Strengthen relationships, marriage and family life and much more.

Our insightful writers provide daily Bible reading notes and other resources for all ages, and our experienced course designers and presenters have gained an international reputation for excellence and effectiveness.

CWR's Training and Conference Centres in Surrey and East Sussex, England, provide excellent facilities in idyllic settings – ideal for both learning and spiritual refreshment.

CWR Applying God's Word
to everyday life and relationships

CWR, Waverley Abbey House,
Waverley Lane, Farnham,
Surrey GU9 8EP, UK

Telephone: **+44 (0)1252 784700**
Email: **info@cwr.org.uk**
Website: **www.cwr.org.uk**

Registered Charity No. 294387
Company Registration No. 1990308